MEMORY LANE

MEMORY LANE
A Photographic Album of Daily Life in Britain
1930-1953

Introduced by James Cameron

Photographic research by Harold Chapman
Captions by Joanna Smith

J. M. Dent & Sons Ltd
London, Melbourne and Toronto

© Introduction, J. M. Dent & Sons Ltd, 1980
Picture selection and text © John Topham Picture Library, 1980

This book is set in VIP Gill Medium by
D. P. Media Limited, Hitchin, Hertfordshire

Printed in Great Britain by
BAS Printers, Stockbridge, Hants for
J. M. Dent & Sons Ltd
Aldine House, 33 Welbeck Street, London

First published in hardback, 1980
Reprinted in hardback and paperback, 1981

British Library Cataloguing in Publication Data

Memory lane.
1. Great Britain – Social life and customs – 20th century – Pictorial works
1. Title
941·083′022′2   DA566·4

ISBN 0-460-04457-5

Pbk ISBN 0-460-02230 x

CONTENTS

The Thirties

Britain at War

The Post-War Years

INTRODUCTION

It is difficult today to think of anyone feeling warmly nostalgic about the 1930s. Some may, but for their own and not history's reasons. It was a bleak and cheerless decade on the whole, and those who remember it – unless they were rich or royal or reckless – do so with the regret that is tempered by time. It took a second World War to bring the grey 1930s to an end; it is a measure of the period that even this seemed – for a moment – a relief.

This is a backhanded way of insisting that an anthology of pictures of the time is uncommonly valuable and important – either as a visual nudge to the memory, or possibly a revelation of how surprisingly prehistoric we seem to have been only a generation ago, in the lifetime of millions of us. Hunger-marchers in 1932 protesting against the Means Test! What on earth was the Means Test? It argued that if an out-of-work family had been provident and diligent enough to have saved up a few quid in better days their dole was harshly cut pro rata. Hospitals existed through charities and flag-days. Pit-workers in privately-owned coal-mines lived like slaves. Barrel-organs – who today has ever seen or heard a barrel-organ, outside the television archives? Splendid steam traction-engines, now to be seen only in museums or at sentimental old crock reunions. All so long ago and far away removed from our contemporary anxieties, this record could seem almost Dickensian, except that to anyone of moderate middle-age they were part of a present and enduring life.

The precursor to this book was called *The Day Before Yesterday*, a photographic album of Victorian and Edwardian Britain, and it was introduced by Peter Quennell. I argue that he had an easier job than mine. His raw material was the hitherto undiscovered country of photography itself, the virgin art of Fox Talbot and Louis Daguerre and Octavius Hill and Francis Frith, and the total novelty and excitement of this pioneering medium made it a revelation.

These old founding fathers had no peers, no criteria; what they made they had created – or, one might technically say, developed. They were essentially craftsmen and artists, and their work was to be wondered at, and even in its infancy to be treasured, because it had never happened before.

Fame was not so easy for their successors. A couple of generations later the medium had become no longer surprising; we were into the age of the amateur snapshot and the diligent newsman; such pictures were no longer for connoisseurs or archivists, and we no longer stood in wonder that people could make photographs at all. By then — and by now — photographs were no longer art, they were communication.

Paradoxically these pictures of the 1930s and 1940s communicate much more to us now than they did then. There could have been nothing particularly novel to the Londoners of the thirties about Covent Garden porters carrying pillars of baskets on their heads; today it would be as odd as seeing the nobs borne around in sedan-chairs. Where have the travelling tinkers gone, and the charcoal-burners? It is not as though we were thinking about flint-knappers or water-diviners or alchemists; these trades and crafts were a normal and accepted part of life a mere forty or so years ago, which makes it all the stranger that in this short span they have already become history.

These pictures of the 1930s and 1940s are rarely distinguished; photography had outpaced the studied soft-focus exposures of the nineteenth century, and photo-journalism was only reaching for the excitement and immediacy it was soon to develop with the memorable *Picture Post* and *Life* magazines. These media, after all, had not yet been born, and the equipment was by our standards slow and square. Even so, often the naiveté and the seemingly casual approach is deeply telling and revealing; it was not always art, but my goodness it was life.

A Britain of the 1980s, mesmerized by contemporary prophecies of impending doom, rarely remembers that it has all been done before. In 1933 there were in the country three million people out of work — a far higher proportion of the population than is the case now. In the United States the *leitmotif* was 'Brother Can You Spare A Dime', and the rhythmic thud on the sidewalk of ruined brokers plunging from Wall Street windows. Most people thought the game was up, and indeed it nearly was. That was some fifty years ago, when you and I were young, laddie.

At least I was, living and working in Dundee, where the staple industry, jute, had collapsed, and where the favourite picture-postcard was an ironic panorama of idle smokeless factory chimneys, captioned 'Bonny Dundee'. As a four pound a week local reporter I was, it seemed, among the well-to-do. If material conditions of life meant anything I was working class, since I worked very hard for little pay, but it did not give me entrance to the confidence of true workers – at least not then – because I was not on the dole. This is precisely the limbo situation which this random anthology of 1930s photographs so memorably encapsulates.

I go on arbitrarily about Dundee, because to me that was the 1930s; 'Jarrow' would be a more evocative word for the period, but there was in fact little difference. I lived in a community of seventy thousand, with some forty thousand of them unemployed. Paradoxically I can find the place represented but once in this collection of pictures – who in the thirties would trouble to photograph an industrial graveyard? – but it was a place of searing ugliness set on a hill and a firth like the Bay of Naples.

This sort of contrast pervaded the Dundee of the 1930s – and many another such stricken town, as the various sections of *Memory Lane* make very clear. It was not only visual, it was social: the opulence of the mill-owners in our suburb of Broughty Ferry, the despairing hovels of our Hilltown slums. I was young and inexperienced, all I could grasp was that this sort of society was wrong, even unnatural, though none of us knew how on earth to oppose it. Political thinking came much later to my generation, though it hummed and throbbed around us the whole time.

It is hard to remember, looking at these scenes of an England inimitably insular both in its back streets and its comfortable country homes, that this in the thirties was a nation on the edge of a continent sliding fast into fascism. In this decade Mussolini and Salazar were joined by Hitler and Franco in an apparently irresistible growth of totalitarianism. Austria and Czechoslovakia vanished into the Third Reich, the Spanish Republic disappeared.

All this has relevance to those who remember the age, however vaguely; it has curiously little to the images in this picture-book – except as a haunting background to every one of them. One would not immediately think that with hindsight so many analysts called the 1930s and early 1940s the Red Decade. It is true that the Communist Party had a membership of 2,500 in 1930, and 17,500 by 1939, and 56,000 by 1942. It was the decade when Victor Gollancz's Left Book Club grew to 58,000 strong. Yet all this was symbolic somehow of despair rather than militant anger; there was little one could do politically, so one joined things, as a gesture of refusal rather than hope. After the disastrous General Strike of 1926 a million trades unionists defected; the Labour Party was deep in the doldrums; after Ramsay MacDonald's sell-out in 1931 it was out of office for the rest of the decade. So one ran about making defiant and wholly useless gestures of solidarity with acceptable people like the Spanish Republicans, the German Jews, and – until the astonishing Hitler-Stalin Pact caught everyone on one foot – the Soviet union.

Although this book is, and very properly, concerned with the small events within our own country – this is in fact its direct and engaging appeal, since these pictures were not taken with posterity in mind – all this domestic trivia must be seen against the background of what Winston Churchill called The Gathering Storm, the not-so-gradual advance of sinister things beyond the frontiers of our insular certainties. The vernal simplicities of these impromptu moments in time – like the touching glimpse of the Maundy Charity in rural Kent – are almost all unrepeatable; already they were vanishing fast, and with absolute certainty will never return.

The great punctuation-mark – certainly of the two decades, possibly of the century – was World War Two, in its way very nearly as dire an illustration of human imbecility as World War One. There is nothing I can say about the Home-Front War that has not been said a thousand times before, and is in any case far better said by these pictures. Its climax, the catastrophic horror of Hiroshima and Nagasaki, made it instantly clear in one thirty-thousandth of a second that scenes like these of the London blitz can never recur in whatever coming Storm the future is Gathering now. Sandbags, barrage balloons, Civil Defence, blackouts – they will all be as useful as the broadsword and buckler against the big bang. I say this with some feeling, since I am one of the very few people who has seen three atom-bombs go off and lived to tell the tale – interminably, I am afraid.

I was called up at the beginning of the War and almost at once kicked out. The army doctors could see no use for me, and enjoined me strictly never again to go above three thousand feet and in no circumstances to have anything to do with the military. Thenceforth I spent years flying at about twenty thousand feet and wearing the uniforms of four armies and navies of different countries in my crazy capacity as war correspondent, an enlightening but not especially ennobling experience.

The wartime photographers were braver than we were. A reporter can fudge his story from other people's stories, a photographer to get his picture has to stand up and be counted, and occasionally killed. He was frequently crippled by a punitive censorship, but he got his prints. Yet the photographers of that time had not yet come to formalize grief, or even, as we did later, to give visual drama to sorrow; there are few pictures of the sort of dramatic despair that we were – and alas are – used to from South East Asia, from Korea, Viet Nam, Kampuchea. I am pretty sure I am right in saying that the 1940s' cameramen were not studied propagandists, as they later became, despite themselves. The technical wheel came full circle, oddly enough. The great men of the nineteenth century were stars by virtue of their own creation – Fox Talbot and Daguerre and Hill and the rest of the innovators. Almost a century had to pass before the craft produced a new and different race of photographic stars – Robert Capa, Don McCullin, Cartier Bresson, Bert Hardy, and countless more – who exploited the creation of the old masters into a new invention of poignant immediacy through their courage, diligence and invention in times of war and torment. Without them, and their colleagues behind the TV movie-cameras, bringing tragedy into everyone's living-room, it is not impossible that Viet Nam would still be going on.

Our present book belongs to neither era, but the lull between. The old masters had come and gone, the new cowboys had yet to arrive on the scene. The age of the gracefully studied Victorian compositions had receded and not yet given place to the swift clip of the firing-squad. What we have here is the essentially persuasive drama of the commonplace – or what passed for the commonplace in our youth. In its way it is far more evocative. None of us were there when my ancestress Julia Margaret took her painstakingly long exposures of Victorian notables; few of us were around when Buddhist monks were burning themselves to death in Saigon. But a lot of us were there when the luckless Edward VIII abdicated the throne of England for the sake of an American divorcee, when water came from wells, when street buskers and musicians had not been conquered by the relentless numbing three-chord thud of the tedious pop guitar. A lot of us still remember pawnshops and public wash-houses, and though fewer of us remember personal gamekeepers and foxhunting we were still around in their time.

These pictures of the 1930s and 1940s abound in ironies that are not, because they could not possibly be, intentional. A post-war Austin factory where all the cars went for export. A Morris Cowley production line with a target of 2,500 vehicles a week. Steel production entirely in private ownership until it was nationalized in 1950, in the face of fierce opposition from the Tories and the House of Lords. The now-banned herring fetching three pounds a cran in Shetland. Bread, never rationed during the war, rationed in peace. Queues for meat, petrol, vegetables, nylons, newspapers. Windmill Girls and Tommy Handley. Seven-inch television sets for a handful of licence holders to watch Philip Harben showing how to cook foods that nobody had. Gertrude Lawrence. Fred Astaire and Ginger Rogers. Schiaparelli and Coco Chanel. The Lambeth Walk. Aneurin Bevan and the National Health. Read all about it. Or rather look at it, and pretend you don't remember.

The Thirties

WORKING

1
Unemployment reached its peak in January 1933, with just under three million out of work.

2
The National Government,
a coalition of Conservatives,
Liberals, and a handful of
Labour MPs, took over from
Labour in 1931 under the
Labour leader Ramsay
MacDonald. It was
confirmed in office by the
election of 1931 and
survived the Depression. In
1935 MacDonald resigned
and Stanley Baldwin took
over the increasingly
Conservative coalition.
Despite the boast of the
1935 election poster, the
economic revival owed little
to Government policies; the
fact was that world prices
were running in Britain's
favour.

▶ 3

Oxford undergraduates with the Lancashire contingent of hunger marchers, protesting against the means test in 1932. Government spending cuts in 1931 included the much-resented means test for those on the dole. Savings and earnings by all members of the family were taken into account and thus hard-working, provident families were penalized.

▶ 4

The Rat and Sparrow Club at Eynsford in Kent, 1939. These clubs, usually paid for by local farmers and based in pubs, gave an opportunity to collect extra cash in convivial surroundings, even if this method of paying for keeping down vermin may appear somewhat barbaric. Members were paid according to the number of vermin tails brought in.

▲ 5
The old suffered much from the Depression and their pensions were too small to allow for an adequate diet. Farnborough provided its old men with a Christmas dinner in 1937.

▶ 6
Girls in this Birmingham school were taught to cope with washday.

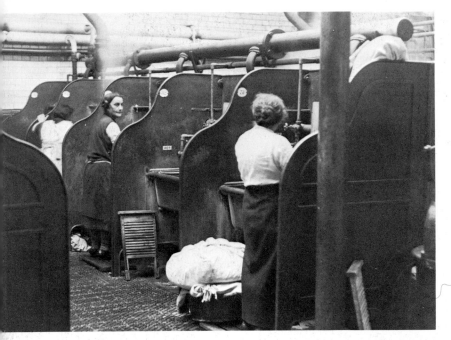

▲ 7
A public wash-house in 1934.
Each cubicle was provided
with hot water (it was
unusual at this time for
working-class homes to have
an indoor water supply) and
a scrubbing board on which
the clothes were rubbed to
get rid of the dirt.

► 8
Monday morning at a
pawnshop in the East End of
London. The women waited
for the pawnshop to open; all
their money had been spent
on Saturday and bundles of
clothes were pawned on
Mondays to be redeemed at
the end of the week if cash
allowed. In one survey it was
found that one family in
three used a pawnbroker.

9
Cap in hand, a villager waits
to receive Maundy peas at
Sutton-at-Hone, Kent, 1933.
This charity dated back to
1572: twenty bushels of peas
and two bushels of wheat
were given to the poor of
the parish every Maundy
Thursday.

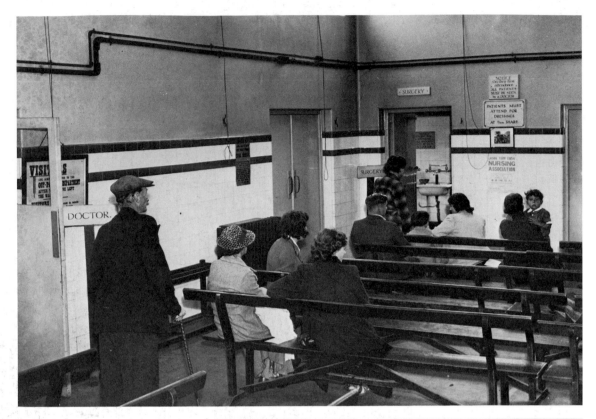

▲ 10
Outpatients Department at
Gravesend Hospital, 1939.
Only wage-earners were
covered by National
Insurance; local authorities
and voluntary organizations
contributed to the cost of
medical treatment for those
in need. Most hospitals were
run by voluntary organ-
izations; money was raised
by bazaars, flag days and
subscriptions.

► 11
An operation in progress,
1939.

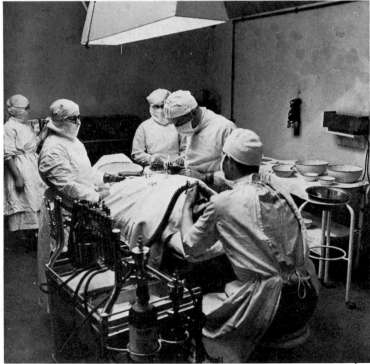

12
The national electricity grid
was almost complete by
1933. Four thousand farms
had electricity in 1932 and
this figure had increased to
30,000 by 1937, although
the pylons were resisted by
conservation groups who
feared the ruin of the English
countryside. The pylons
could be equally obtrusive in
the towns. This pylon was
sited in a suburban garden.

13
Electricity was a boon to the housewife who could afford this electric washing machine.

14
Magnificent machinery at a waterworks in 1939; but many households in towns and entire rural communities were still without mains water.

15
The gas cleaner, Gravesend Gas-works.

◀ **16**
Manufacturing methods were frequently primitive. Here a worker pours sulphuric acid onto cadmium bars at the Tyke and Kings Chemical Works, 1936.

◀ **17**
A general view of the chemical works.

◀ **18**
The coal miners were hard hit by the Depression. Many mines closed and others worked irregularly; the work was hard and conditions often appalling. These miners are taking coal home on their bicycles, 1936.

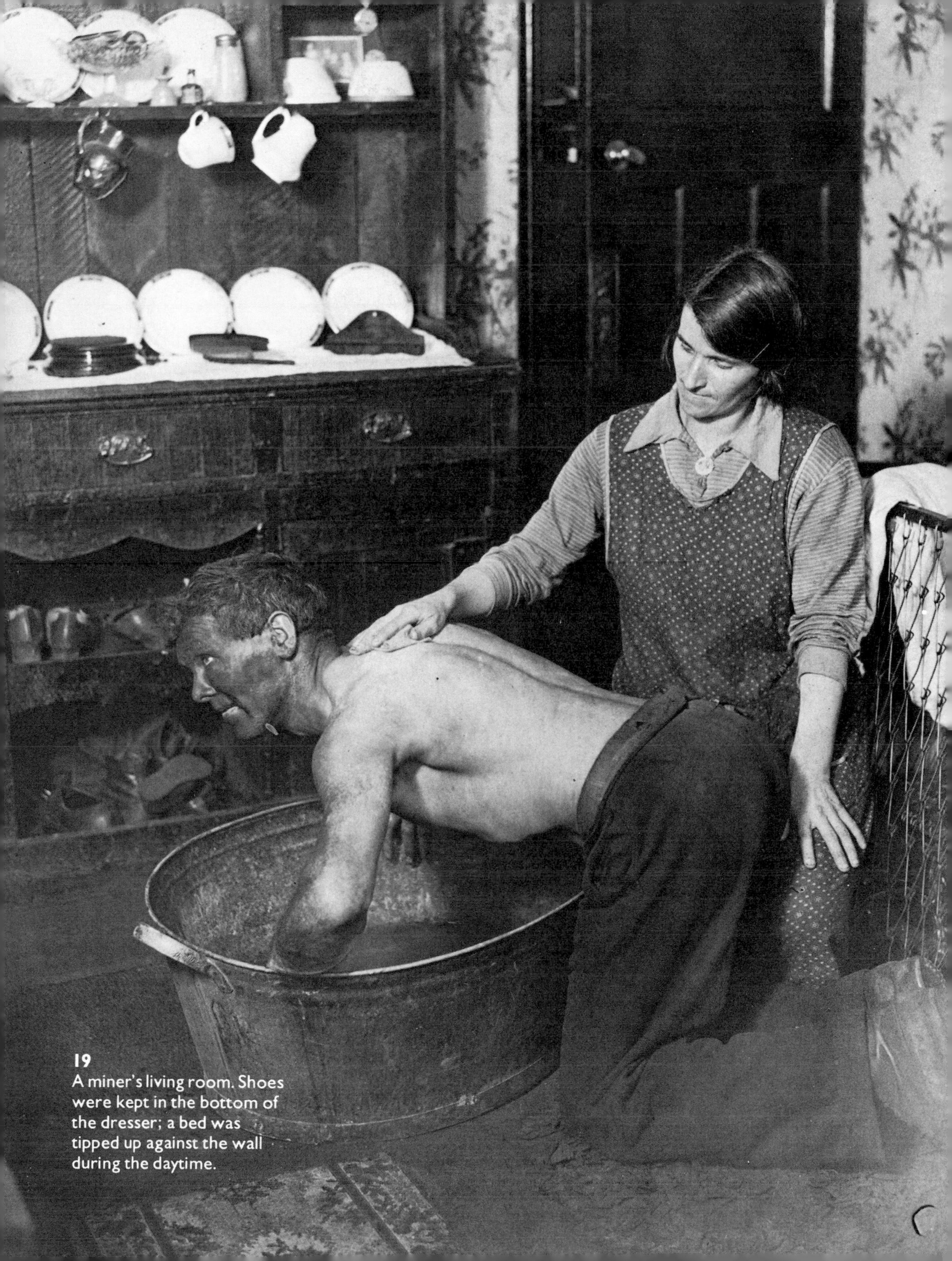

19
A miner's living room. Shoes
were kept in the bottom of
the dresser; a bed was
tipped up against the wall
during the daytime.

◀ **20**
Few workers possessed
alarm clocks, so the services
of this 'knocker up' were in
demand. She woke her
clients by shooting peas at
their windows.

▼ **21**
Factory tea boys, 1938.

▶ **22**
A job at sea had its attractions. This was the captain's table aboard a tramp steamer in 1936.

▼ **23**
Tea break on a shrimping boat, 1936.

◄ 24

Most homes were still heated by a single coal fire in the living room and deliveries of coal were a common sight. The coal was often tipped through a hole or down a chute into a coal store in the basement, as in this photograph.

► 25

Van drivers.

▼ 26

A milkman and his Bedford van.

L.PAPA & SON'S
DIPLOMA ICE CREAM.

◄ 31
A travelling salesman, Devon 1935.

► 32
Road sweepers' dinner, winter 1935.

▼ 33
Barrel Organ depot, Stepney 1933. The Italian /Cockney owner hired out the barrel organs, and the price varied from a shilling to half-a-crown a day, depending on the number of tunes that the organ could play.

◄ **34**
'Whistling Rufus', the street musician, with a penny whistle, 1937.

▼ **35**
A barrel organ far from home, 1934.

ON THE STREET

The city streets of the thirties were often squalid but teeming with interest and vitality, not yet impersonalized by the motor car, smelling of horses and manure. The horses were often led through the terraced houses to their stables in the backyards.

36
Police remove an alcoholic
by police ambulance, 1931.

◄ **37**
Sailing ships could still be
seen in the docks, 1933.

▲ **38**
A toll gate in East London.

► **39**
The drama of a runaway
horse provided occasional
excitement.

◀ **40**
A street in Limehouse, 1933, since demolished. Women sat out on the pavement on warm days.

◀ **41**
Children and toddlers played in the street; even a child of this age could be allowed to play outside, wander off and come back in the care of the policeman on the beat.

▲ **42**
There were few toys; the street urchins found their own amusements.

▲ **43**
Children in Wapping, 1933.

◀ **44**
A home-made puppet
theatre.

▲ **45**
An Indian toffee-seller.

46
A mobile fun fair, with miniature merry-go-round and a bugle-blowing operator.

▲ 47
As few people had cars, trade deliveries were commonplace.

◄ 48
By 1938 road traffic and road accidents had much increased and the children were no longer able to play in the streets.

► **49**

Boy Scouts built this monster bonfire for King George V's Jubilee in 1935, which was an astonishing display of loyalty and affection. In his Jubilee broadcast the King, deeply moved, said, 'How can I express what is in my heart? . . . I can only say to you, my very dear people, that the Queen and I thank you from the depths of our hearts for all the loyalty and – may I say? – the love with which this day and always you have surrounded us.'

▼ **50**

Loyalty to the Crown survived the Abdication of Edward VIII and street parties such as this were given to celebrate George VI's coronation.

GETTING ABOUT

51
Road gives way to river:
Tower Bridge 1933.

▲ 52
London and North Eastern
Railway cart-horse availing
itself of a Metropolitan
water trough, 1939.

53
Horse-drawn traffic on
London Bridge in the
thirties.

54
Tricycles were a boon to the old and unsteady.

◄ **55**
Women waving to a steamer at London Docks in 1934. Boats and trains still carried most Britons on long-distance journeys.

▲ 56
Re-gilding the lettering on
Euston Station's late-
lamented Doric arch, 1933.

◀ **57**
Bank Holiday traffic on the Kingston By-pass, which had been opened in 1927.

◀ **58**
A drive in the country, 1938. There were almost two million private cars in Britain by 1939.

▶ **59**
Country roads were almost empty of traffic. Here in 1936 a car passes a horse-drawn mower.

◄ 60
At a country garage apples
were given to customers,
1936. Petrol was 1s. 4d.
(roughly 7p) a gallon.

▲ 61
A police car in 1933.

◄ 62
With no driving test for motorists and no speed limit in built-up areas until 1934, road traffic took a heavy toll. This animal cemetery was in Hildenborough.

◄ 63
Children practising for a road safety demonstration at the National Safety First Congress at Westminster in 1939.

▲ 64
Few new roads were built in
the thirties. This German
mechanical navvy was used
on the new Mickleham
By-pass.

65
Building the Dartford Tunnel,
January 1938.

▲ 66
The airship *Graf Zeppelin*
landing at Hanworth in
1931. The British airship
R101 had burst into flames
at Beauvais on a test flight to
India in 1930, killing 48
people. The Germans
operated a trans- atlantic
airship service from 1936
until the *Hindenburg* was
destroyed by fire on its
maiden flight, May 1937.
After this disaster attempts
to develop airships were
finally abandoned.

▼ 67

Nannies and their charges
on the banks of the Medway
at Rochester, September
1937. The flying boat was
one of the Empire Class,
'Cambria'. These aircraft
flew the luxury overseas
routes of Imperial Airways
and were the forerunners of
the Sunderland Flying Boats.
The Short Bros. Aircraft
Works were based at this
spot from 1913 until they
were moved to Belfast in
1947, having suffered
heavily from war damage.

▲ **68**
Empire Air Day, Biggin Hill,
1937.

▶ **69**
Amy Johnson after a crash in
1936, when she was flying
solo from Paris to London.

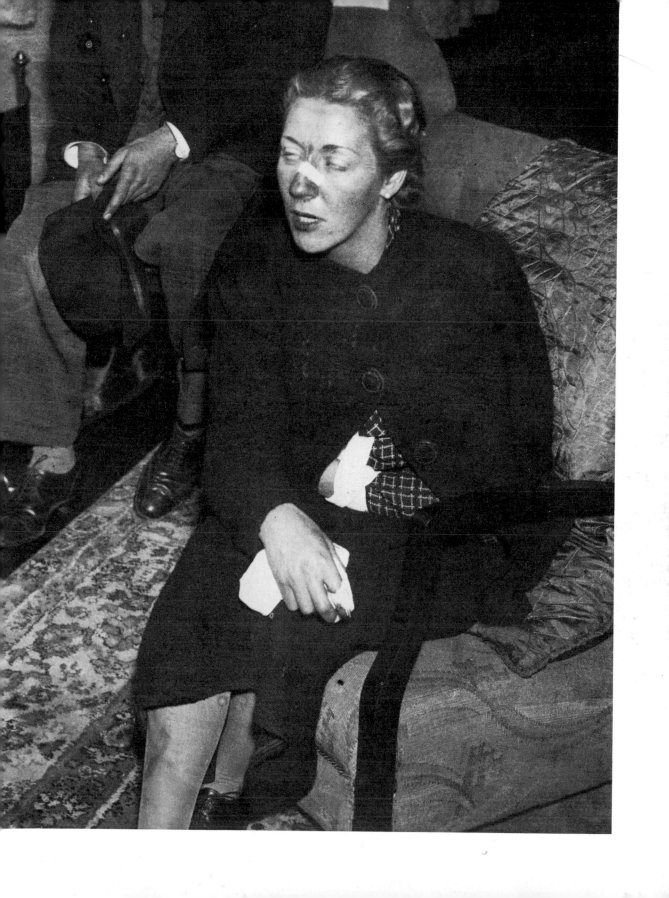

IN THE COUNTRY

◄ **70**
Hens still scratched around
the farmyards and country
people still woke to the
sound of cocks crowing.

▲ **71**
Once the entrance to a
stately home, this archway
spanned the Norwich–
Aylsham road. The lodge
beside it had been
converted into a post office.

▲ 72
A farm labourer in
Orpington, 1935, driving his
cart into the water to swell
the wood and thus tighten
the wheels.

▲ **73**
This well was the only
source of water for the
Kentish village of Dean
Bottom in 1939.

▲ **74**
The lady of the manor: Mrs Sacheverell Sitwell at her house near Towcester in Northamptonshire.

▶ **75**
A country gamekeeper, dressed in breeches and leather gaiters, with his 'gibbet'. These macabre displays of destroyed vermin and predators were once a common sight. Behind the keeper can be seen his coops for pheasant-rearing.

76
The hunt moving off down
Bletchingley's village street,
1936. At this date rides were
kept open by landlords and
farmers, who often hunted
themselves, while hedges
had not yet been replaced by
barbed wire to any great
extent.

▶ **79**
Hoeing turnips in
Kirkcudbrightshire,
Scotland, 1933.

80
Dung-spreading in February
1939.

81
Steam threshing-machines
travelled from farm to farm.
Water for the engine was
brought from the nearest
pond by horse and cart. The
carefully built cornstacks
were dismantled as sheaf
after sheaf was passed into
the machine. Threshing was
a winter job; this
photograph was taken in
February 1936.

◀ 82

Lambing time 1935.
Shepherds camped by
their flocks; many used
Old English sheepdogs.

▼ 83

A watercress grower,
wearing rubber waders,
1938. Rubber boots
contributed perhaps more
than anything else to the
comfort of country
workers.

84
Milk churn collection in
Staffordshire, 1937. Farmers
used to drive with their milk
churns to their local railway
stations but by about 1930
the churns were picked up
by lorries and taken to a
creamery.

▲ **85**
Ploughing in 1937.

▼ **86**
Bagging up potatoes from a
vast clamp. Scotland 1939.

87
Skilled men walked the hopfields on huge stilts to string the hop poles. Kent, 1937.

88
Canterbury cattle market in 1936 provided entertainment for free.

◀ **89**
A village baby show in 1936.

▼ **90**
Basket-makers at Swanley,
1936.

91
Londoners came to the
country for the hop-picking.

◀ **92**
Hoppers' picnic in the hop
garden.

▼ **93**
Fat lambs for the London
market, July 1937.

◄ 94
A travelling tinker in 1937,
with his goods in a battered
perambulator.

▲ 95
A charcoal burner's hut,
1935.

96
The cinema was at the peak of its popularity in the thirties; 40 per cent of the population went to the cinema once a week and 25 per cent went twice a week or more.

97
George VI, then the Duke of York, took his wife and daughters to the Pantomime *Dick Whittington* at the Lyceum, 1935.

◀ 99
Fred Astaire and Ginger Rogers danced together in many films, including *The Gay Divorcee* and *Top Hat*. Their partnership followed a successful brother-sister dancing team which Fred and his sister Adèle maintained for twenty-five years, until 1932.

▼ 100
The comedienne Cicely Courtneidge, who was singing 'All the King's Horses' in the early thirties.

◀ 98
Actors and actresses such as Gertrude Lawrence, Noël Coward and Ivor Novello dominated the stage in London in the 1930s.

◄ 101
A seaside holiday was
popular with rich and poor.
Princess Alexandra, Prince
Edward and nannies left
Belgrave Square for
Sandwich, July 1938.

▼ 102
East-enders took home-
made go-carts to Gravesend.

103
Mrs Andrews of Sidcup
went to Brighton for
the day in July
1937. She had never
been more than six
miles from her home
before.

104
Butlin's Holiday Camp; the
first was opened at Skegness
in 1937.

▲ 105
A 'Keep Fit' craze swept the nation. Bexley Heath opened its public swimming bath in typical English weather, 1936.

▶ 106
Cycling became a popular sport. These cyclists had been bluebell-gathering.

▲ 107
Litter became a problem in the rural beauty spots and there were anti-litter campaigns.

▶ 108
The zoo was a perennial favourite and some exciting buildings went up in the thirties such as the Penguin Park at London Zoo (1933–4). Princess Elizabeth was allowed to go for a walk down the ramp with the penguins on a visit in 1938.

◀ 109
Gambling, on the pools, greyhound-racing and horse-racing, was the chief vice and excitement of the thirties. By 1931 there were eighteen million attendances at greyhound racing tracks.

◀ 110
Moralists were shocked that women, too 'went to the dogs'.

▶ 111
The 'tote' at Hurst Park, 1939. Totalisators encouraged small betting and helped horse-racing hold its own against the competition from the greyhound tracks.

112
Sir Malcolm Campbell, with his new *Bluebird* in 1933. In the cockpit is his son, Donald. Malcolm Campbell was knighted in 1931 when he returned from Florida where he had set a new land speed record of 246.09 m.p.h. in the 1,400 h.p. *Bluebird*. Later *Bluebird* was given a 2,250 h.p. Rolls Royce engine. Campbell's highest speed was 301.13 m.p.h. at Bonneville, Utah in 1935.

113
Campbell, seen here talking to schoolboys, was one of the heroes of the thirties; others were Amy Johnson who flew solo to Australia in 1930, the Australian cricketer Don Bradman, Fred Perry who won the men's title at Wimbledon 1934, 1935 and 1936 and Len Hutton who scored a record-breaking 364 runs in the Test Match against the Australians, 1938, at the tender age of twenty-two.

◀ 114
A quieter, but popular,
competitive sport was
pigeon-racing. Pigeons,
transported by rail, were
liberated by the station
master for the race.

▲ 115
A Schiaparelli model, 1937.
Elsa Schiaparelli, with Coco
Chanel, dominated the Paris
fashion world in the thirties;
she was the first to use
artificial fabrics for her
dresses.

▲ 116
Eton boys in a tea shop.

▶ 117
A country pub, 1931.

◀ **118**
   1932 Bank holiday, Dartford
   Paddling Pool.

▼ **119**
   The Duke and Duchess of
   Windsor after their
   wedding, 3 June 1937.

◄ 120
The light music and dance
tunes of the thirties came
mainly from America.

▲ 121
Buying gramophone
records with the help of
hand-held earphones.

122
Jitterbugging, which came over from America in 1939. It never achieved the success of the Lambeth Walk, Christmas 1937, which sold more copies than any tune since 'Yes We Have No Bananas'.

123
A Fascist meeting at Chiswick. The British Union of Fascists was formed under Oswald Mosley's leadership early in 1932; it reached its peak of success in 1934, with an estimated 20,000 members. A mass rally at Olympia in June 1934, at which opponents were ejected with considerable brutality, and disquieting events in Hitler's Fascist Germany eroded support for Mosley and his party.

◀ **124**
Oswald Mosley (second from left) in 1932, the year that his book *The Greater Britain* was published.

▼ **125**
Armistice memorial service, 1938. Within two years many of the 1914–18 veterans would enlist in the Home Guard and prepare to resist invasion.

126
A Hawker Demon on a
training flight over the
Medway at Rochester, 1938.

127
A giant bomber preparing to
take off before a large
crowd at Biggin Hill, Empire
Air Day, 1937.

◀ **128**
The Czechoslovakia crisis,
March 1938. Demonstrators
outside the German Embassy
in Carlton House Terrace.

▼ **129**
May, 1938. Air Defence of
London searchlights giving a
display outside the Odeon
cinema, Wellhall.

▲ 130
6 September 1938. The
balloon barrage was
demonstrated to Sir
Kingsley Wood, the Air
Minister, at Kidbrooke. By
late September most people
in Britain expected that war
would be declared within a
day or two.

▶ 131
Appeasement: Chamberlain
arrives at Heston after his
meeting with Hitler,
September 1938.

INSPECTION OF THE CORRESPON

E COLUMN

132
David Low's caustic cartoon
on the Munich Agreement
and 'Peace with honour'.

133
April 1938. The final tableau
at a National Service
Recruiting Campaign at the
Royal Cinema, Bexleyheath.

◀ **134**
September 1939. The curate of Horsmonden acting as postman during the crisis over Poland.

◀ **135**
'We're gonna hang out the washing on the Siegfried Line' on permanent display at a London nightclub. War had come at last.

Britain at War

BRITAIN PREPARES

136
The end of appeasement:
the German Army invaded
Poland on 1 September
1939; Britain and France
declared war on Germany
two days later.

137
The Queen's broadcast to
the nation on 12 September
1939.

138
The expected bombs did not
fall during the Twilight War,
or the Phoney War as it was
dubbed by the Americans; a
peaceful scene in Trafalgar
Square as people sat in the
sun, near the air raid shelter
and the powerful loud-
speaker system.

◀ **139**
Business as usual behind a wall of sandbags at the Kardomah. The photograph was taken through a spy hole, as people using cameras ran the risk of being arrested.

◀ **140**
Telephone directories and sandbags were used to defend the Sidcup Post Office.

141
Householders were kept
busy even at night. By
paraffin lamplight, they filled
sandbags and buckets of
sand to protect houses from
blast and to put out fires.
Rose Macaulay wrote at the
time: 'I think this is a good
thing, as it gives people
something they feel useful
to do.' The hole created
might be used for an air raid
shelter.

GOVERNMENT EVACUATION SCHEME

The Government have ordered evacuation of registered school children.

If your children are registered, visit their assembly point at once and read the instructions on the notice board.

The name and address of the assembly point is given on the notice to parents.

Posters notifying arrival will be displayed at the schools at which the children assemble for evacuation.

The County Hall,
S.E.I

E. M. RICH,
Education Officer

▲ 142
The war scare at the time of Munich had given the authorities useful experience in evacuating children. Between 1 and 3 September 1939, 1,500,000 mothers and children were evacuated from London with a minimum of fuss.

▶ 143
The evacuees were not told their destination. These bewildered children, labelled, carrying gas masks and luggage — a change of clothes, nightclothes, washing things and if possible a warm coat or mackintosh — had just arrived at Eastbourne on I September. The children tended to settle down better in their new homes when they moved with their teachers and their mothers stayed behind.

144
Refreshment for the evacuees.

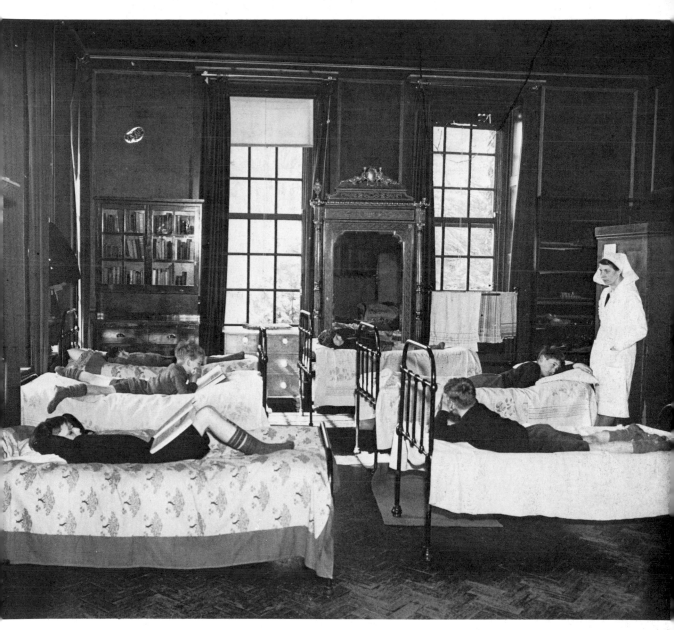

JOINING UP

▲ 147
Conscription, which had
been resisted by the Labour
and Liberal parties in 1938,
finally came into full effect in
1939, when it was intro-
duced for men between the
ages of eighteen and
forty-one.

▶ 148
For the older generation,
with their memories of
1914, the outbreak of a
second World War brought
terrible anxiety. The
photographer caught the
Vicar of Sidcup saying
goodbye to his son, a
volunteer in the Artists
Rifles, on 3 September 1939.

▲ 149
On 10 May 1940, Germany
invaded Holland and
Belgium. While the
placards read 'Heavy Firing
on West Front', a blood
transfusion service was
being organized in London.

▶ 150
Dutch and Belgian
refugees began to arrive in
England.

◀ 151
British soldiers (the C.O.
and officers of the Royal
Ulster Rifles) waiting on
an improvised pier near
Dunkirk for a boat to take
them to England and safety.
Almost all the British Army
equipment and ammunition
was left behind, but the
huge majority of the
Expeditionary Force was
rescued. The boats which
went out to Dunkirk
included the Gravesend
steamer which had been
used to evacuate some of
London's children.

▲ 152
Battle of Britain pilots from
Biggin Hill spent many
off-duty hours in the White
Hart, Brasted, where the
board on which they signed
their names can still be seen.

LUNCHEONS.

THE BEACH

153
The Clarendon Hotel in
Deal was used as an army
canteen (1943).

▲ 154
Pacifists and conscientious
objectors were not treated
as badly as they had been in
the First World War.
Almost 44,000 'conchies'
were given exemption. The
Pacifist magazine, *Peace
News*, was on sale here in
1944.

▶ 155
America and Germany were
at war from 11 December
1941, but American
servicemen did not arrive in
Britain in force until 1943.
American Military Police in
Piccadilly, 1943.

▲ **156**
American airforcemen
having a final pint in their
local before leaving England
in 1945.

▶ **157**
A sad farewell between an
American air-force sergeant
and his girlfriend, a British
aircraftwoman. Many US
servicemen married British
girls.

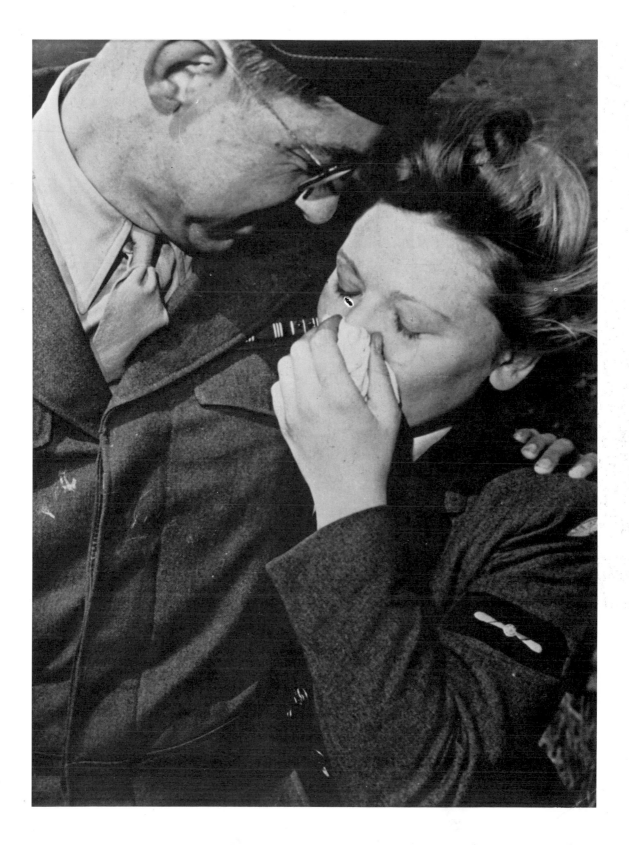

BRITAIN ALONE

158
On 14 May 1940 Anthony Eden broadcast an appeal for citizens between the ages of fifteen and sixty-five to join the Local Defence Volunteers (the LDV), soon to be renamed the Home Guard. In six weeks a million men had enrolled; more than 50 per cent had served in the First World War.

159
In the early days of the
Home Guard there was only
one gun for every ten men.
Volunteers drilled in civilian
clothes, carrying sticks.
America sent 800,000 rifles
in the summer of 1940;
there was then one rifle to
every three men and there
was also an assortment of
grenades, shot-guns and
Brownings.

160
The board outside
Gravesend Parish Church,
1940. All place-names which
could have helped invading
troops were removed by
Government order in May
1940 and in case of invasion
the church bells would ring.
On 7 September it was
assumed that the invasion
had begun, the church bells
rang out their warning and
some attempts were made
to blow up bridges and
railway stations before it
was realized that it was a
false alarm.

161
Old cars were strung across
fields so that they could not
be used as landing grounds
by enemy aircraft.

◄ **162**

Trenches were dug in the Kentish hopfields so that pickers and their families could take refuge during the Battle of Britain. *Life* magazine said, 'This is the most human picture of the war' and it was displayed, greatly enlarged, in the British Embassy in Washington.

▼ **163**

Firemen and wardens trained the public to use stirrup pumps. Here the Poet Laureate, John Masefield, was learning to use the nozzle which could be adjusted either to spray an incendiary bomb or to direct a jet at a fire. Three people were needed: one used the nozzle, one did the pumping and one fetched fresh water supplies.

◄ 164

By early September 1939 a million and a half Anderson shelters (named after Sir John Anderson) had been distributed in London, free of charge to those whose income was below £250 a year. They were sunk three feet into the ground, and many people used the roof to grow flowers or vegetables. They saved many lives; of Londoners who used shelters, more than half used Anderson shelters.

▲ 165

This seventy-six-year-old pensioner made a shelter thirty feet long, twelve feet below ground, covered by a mound of earth and concrete eight feet high. He provided seats for twenty people and installed electric light; he constructed the whole thing entirely on his own.

▼ 166
Flying glass was a real danger: the owner of this house used paper cake mats to make the windows splinter proof.

▶ 167
Of all air raid precautions, the blackout caused the greatest inconvenience and hardship. Blackout houses were hot and stuffy in summer and often had to remain dark all day.

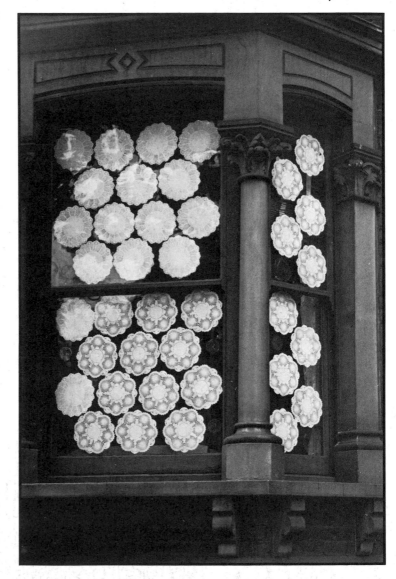

▼ **168**
Road accidents were, not
unnaturally, common in the
blackout. Pedestrians were
advised to wear white, or
smoke so that they could be
seen. Luminous flowers
were an ingenious answer
to the problem.

► **169**
Wardens were enrolled, both men and women. Between three and six wardens belonged to each wardens' post and were responsible for a district of about five hundred people. They had to make sure blackout regulations were observed, check gas masks, train the public to deal with incendiary bombs, report bomb damage and give warning in case of bomb attack.

▲ 170
Empty houses were
commandeered for all kinds
of uses – first aid posts, fire
alarm stations, billets for
soldiers. Trees with white
circles were blackout aids.

▶ 171
No one who heard the wail
of the air raid warning siren
will ever forget the sound.
Wailing Winnie, flying the
Union Jack, was in South
London.

THE BLITZ

172
Wardens, resented in early
days for their bossiness (it
was rumoured that they
spent their time playing
darts) came into their own
when the Blitz began in
earnest on 7 September
1940.

▲ 173
Unexploded bombs landed
in the most surprising places
and had to be defused – by
the end of the war more
than 50,000 unexploded
bombs had been dealt with.

▶ 174
Between September 1940
and May 1941 20,000
Londoners were killed and
70,000 injured, 25,000
seriously. In the rest of
Britain a further 23,000 died.
Few pictures like this were
taken as there was no
chance of the censor
allowing publication;
propaganda pictures were
more common.

175
Churchill inspecting air raid damage in Battersea, September 1940.

▲ 176
Casualty and rescue
workers in Manchester
1940.

▶ 177
The damaged High Altar and
gaping roof of St Paul's
Cathedral after an air raid in
October 1940.

◄ **178**
London, due to its size,
could continue to function
through the worst that the
bombs could do, but the
devastation was terrifying.
By the end of May 1941 one
in six Londoners had been
made homeless at one time
or another. The worst raid
on London was on 10 May
1941 when 1,450 people
died and the Tower,
Westminster Abbey and the
House of Commons were
hit. This was the scene in
Piccadilly.

▲ **179**
Coventry, 14 November
1940 gave a new word to
the German language –
'Coventrieren' or
'Coventrate'.

180
The flying bomb attacks
(V1) on London began after
the Normandy landings on
13 June 1944. Many were
shot down before they
reached their target, but
two-thirds got through.
Rockets like this V2 began
to arrive on 8 September
1944. Hitler's 'secret
weapon' gave no warning of
its approach and as Harold
Macmillan said with
understatement 'it was
indeed fortunate that they
were not perfected sooner'.
The rockets were
eventually halted when their
bases were overrun by the
advancing Allied troops.

181
Wartime wedding. The
reception was held in the air
raid shelter.

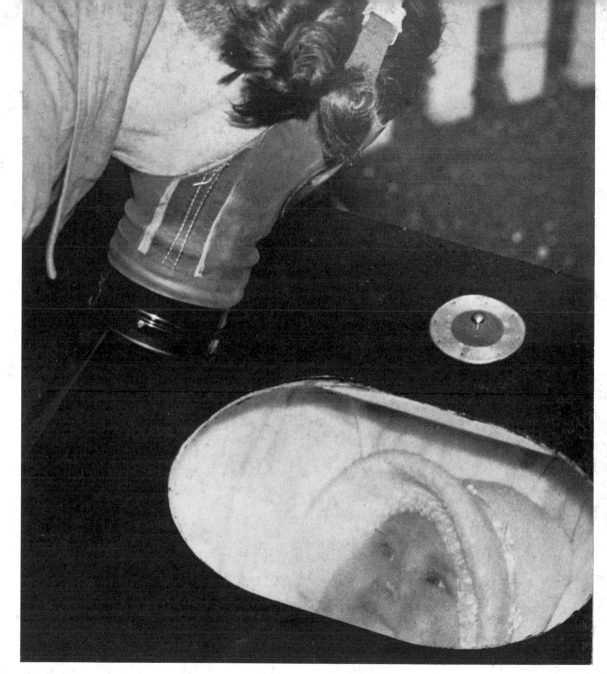

◀ **182**
At the outbreak of war, the chief fear had been of gas attack and gas masks were distributed by all available means.

▲ **183**
Gas-proof containers were made for children too young to wear masks.

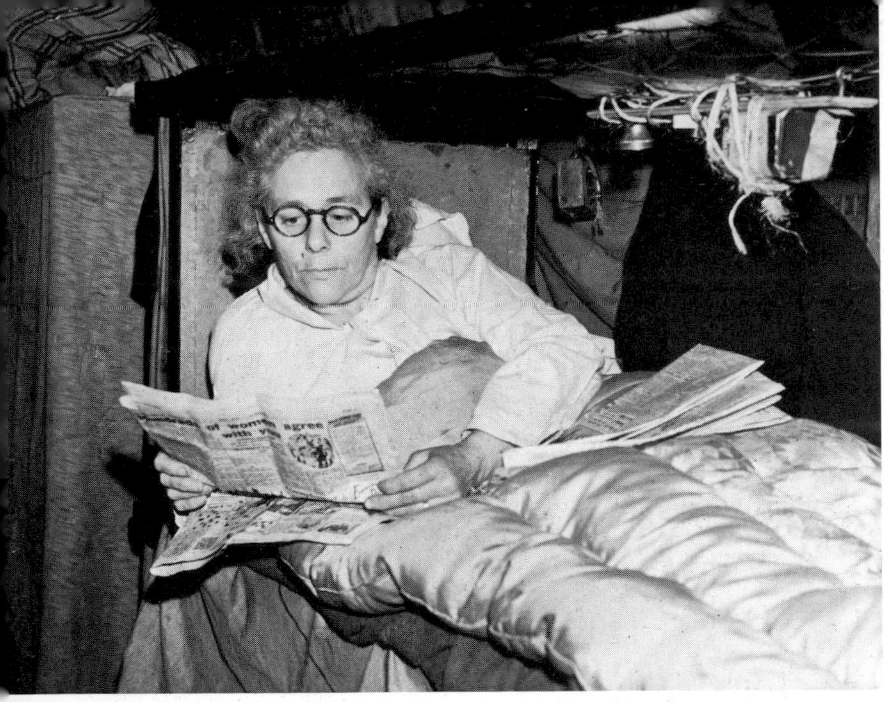

◀ **184**
When the bombing started in earnest, the air raid shelter became a way of life. Bunks, eiderdowns, reading lights, warmth and company helped to make the nights tolerable.

▼ **185**
Christmas in Oxford Street shelter, 1940.

▶ **186**
The tube station at the British Museum was used as a children's play centre as well as an air raid shelter.

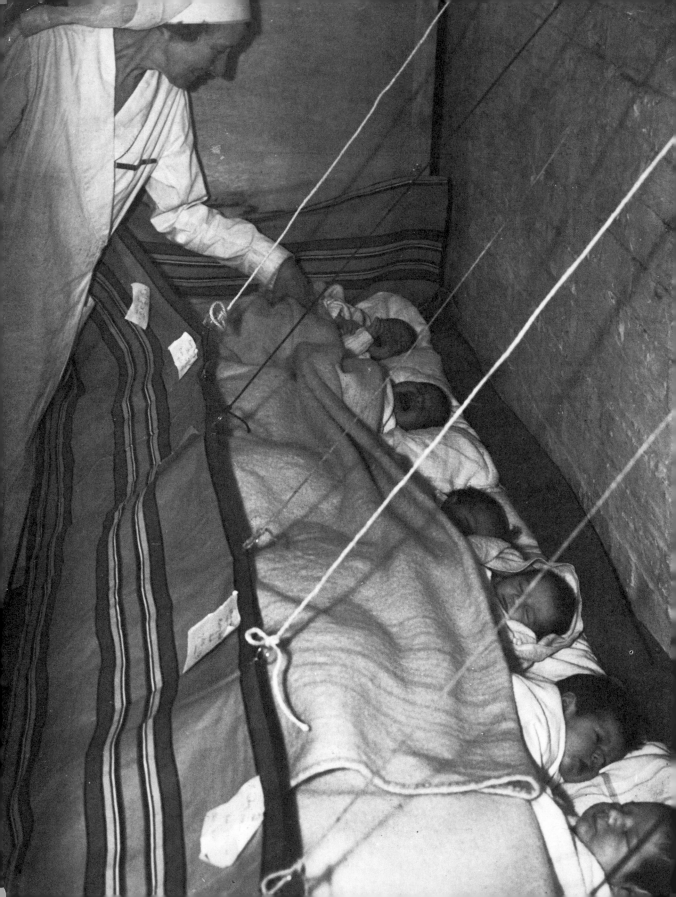

◀ **187**

A rack of babies at Richmond Hospital shelter.

▶ **188**

A woman driver of a double-decker bus in Oxford. The demands of war on manpower were at first masked by the large numbers of unemployed. There were still 1⅓ million unemployed in Britain in January 1940. But by spring 1942 all the available men had been absorbed. Women took a number of jobs as they had in the First World War.

▲ 192
Manpower was not the only
shortage. Bones were
salvaged to make glue for
aircraft; aluminium kettles
and saucepans were
collected to make Spitfires.

▶ 193
To make the food go round,
eating habits had to change.
It was reluctantly accepted
that crops for direct human
consumption had ten times
the food value of meat
reared on the same tonnage
of cereals. Accordingly
almost four million acres
were ploughed up between
1939 and 1941; this worker
was clearing Feltwell Fen in
Norfolk.

◀ **194**
   The omnivorous pig, fed on
swill made from waste, was
a comparatively efficient
meat producer and pig clubs
became a craze, even in
cities. King George VI posed
for a propaganda
photograph.

▲ **195**
   Queen Mary, at her wartime
home at Badminton, set a
good example in land
clearance for cultivation.
She was seventy-five when
this photograph was taken
in 1942.

RELAXATION

◀ 196
Lady Violet Bonham-Carter
in 1944. Difficulties with
petrol and the blackout
meant that people tended to
spend their evenings at
home. There was no
television in wartime but the
radio was turned on for the
six o'clock news in most
homes.

▲ 197
Radio also provided
entertainment, notably
Tommy Handley's *ITMA*
(It's That Man Again) which
probably did more for
morale than the
government propaganda.

198
The Brains Trust first
broadcast in 1941 and
continued throughout the
war. A panel of three men,
the philosopher Professor
C.E.M. Joad (shown here),
the scientist Julian Huxley
and Commander Campbell,
answered questions sent in
by listeners.

▲ 199
Harry Lauder at home.

▶ 200
Deborah Kerr.

201
Pin-up girls 1943.

202
Many entertainers took to
the road to bring cheer to
troops stationed all over
Britain. Here Hughie Green
is shown with his bus which
he drove himself.

◀ 203
A 1943 hit song by the
Andrews Sisters was 'The
Zoot Suit' after a craze for
these bizarre garments
swept America.

▶ 204
Covent Garden Opera
House was turned into a
dance hall.

▶ 205
There was a marked
increase in the demand for
books. Longmans published
The Shelter Book in 1940, an
anthology to keep
shelterers company in 'the
life of huddle and hard bunks
. . . improvised sanitation,
vacuum flasks, torches,
community singing'.

206
Few motor cars, many
pedestrians in Newcastle
upon Tyne, 1945.

207
1945 brought victory at last —
but American aid was cut off
on 17 August and lend-lease,
at Truman's direction, ended
on VJ day. The outlook for
Britain was bleak.

The Post-War Years

A ROOF OVER ONE'S HEAD

208
The war made thousands
homeless. As the men were
demobilized and came back,
bitterness grew. Squatters,
supported by a vigorous
campaign by the Communist
party, moved into empty
properties all over London
in large numbers. As fast as
they were evicted, they
settled elsewhere.

209
The empty military camps
and gun sites were tempting
homes for squatters.
Twenty thousand people
moved into derelict camps
in 1946. Eventually the
Government accepted their
presence and six thousand
families were allowed to
stay. No less than 563
camps, full of squatters,
were handed over to the
local authorities.

210
Self-help in Birmingham. In 1949 fifty families joined forces to build their own bungalows. While the men worked on bricklaying, wives made tea and cooked in the site hut.

211
A septuagenarian Suffolk couple housed themselves in a converted trolley bus, parked in a field. They foiled the Council's attempts to move them by thatching the roof of their bus, thus changing it from a 'mobile home' into a 'permanent dwelling'.

213
Wapping 1950, in London's
East End. These flats had
been built in the 1890s for
workers building Tower
Bridge.

◀ **214**
More than 60,000 houses were built in 1945 and 1946. Two-thirds of these were 'prefabs'.

◀ **215**
There were Prefab Garden Competitions. Here is the winner of the 1948 Queen Mary Cup, Police Sergeant Botwright of Camberwell.

◀ **216**
This family were able to beat food shortages by producing vegetables, chickens and rabbits in their prefab garden.

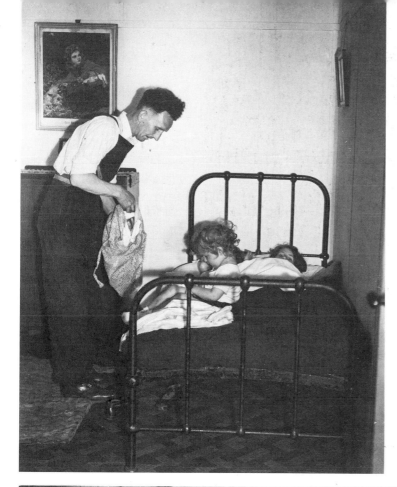

◀ 217
With its two bedrooms, the prefab was rather cramped for this family with three children.

▼ 218
The living room, however, was made comfortable with furniture salvaged from the family's previous home, which had been bombed.

219
The lucky few obtained council flats. This block in Chelsea was built in 1948 and was considered luxurious. Each flat had three bedrooms, a living room, kitchen and bathroom and the rent was 16s. 6d. a week.

▶ 220
These flats in Paddington were also completed in 1948. They boasted 'all the latest household amenities', such as hot and cold running water in each flat, central heating, refrigerators, and power points throughout.

▼ 221
1946: a Housing Office in Holborn.

◀ 222
A housing lottery in Erith,
Kent; 1,300 hopefuls drew
for the 120 houses available.

▼ 223
Much of the housing
remained woefully
inadequate. In the mid-
1950s there was no bath-
room for this family and the
washstand was shared with
three other families. There
was no running hot water.

◀ **224**
The same family at tea-time. To save space in their all-purpose room, there were only four chairs for a family of six.

◀ **225**
The Salvation Army raised money to help the destitute.

▼ 226

Salvation Army Cadets at a men's lodging place at Manor House, Camberwell. In 1949 the Army provided a bed for 10,000 men every night of the year. Their slogan for 1950 was 'Go for souls and go for the worst!'

▲ 227
In the country, gipsy families kept to their old ways. Painted horse-drawn caravans could still be seen by the side of the road, with hobbled, skewbald horses grazing nearby. For a livelihood, gipsies relied on seasonal work on the land.

▶ 228
A farmhouse tea in Wales, 1950. The house was lit with 'bottled gas' and salt pork hung from the ceiling.

229
The open fire, soon to be banished by affluence and Clean Air regulations, was still the main source of heat for British houses in the forties. Central heating was rarely to be found, and the British, accustomed to hard winters and draughty homes, often found centrally-heated buildings oppressive and unhealthy.

GETTING BACK TO WORK

In 1945 British exports were less than half of the pre-war figure and government expenditure abroad was four times as great as before the war. The country was heavily in debt, industry was badly run down and vast sums were needed to reclothe, feed and house the people. The Labour government was planning the nationalization of key industries and the introduction of the Welfare State.

230
Exports were the chief priority. Austin cars went overseas while at home people nursed their old cars or did without.

◄ 231
The production line at the
Morris Cowley factory in
Oxford, 1946. The target
was 2,500 cars a week.

▼ 232
The coal mines were
nationalized on 1 January
1947, but the miners were
disillusioned to find that
conditions were slow to
change.

THIS COLLIERY IS NOW
MANAGED BY THE
NATIONAL
COAL BOARD
ON BEHALF OF THE PEOPLE

 235
Steel at Corby, 1946. Steel was finally nationalized in 1950 in the face of bitter opposition from the Conservatives, aided by the House of Lords.

▶ **236**
Twenty-four seater helicopter at the Farnborough Show, 1949.

▲ **237**
Barrels for the Shetland catch of herring being unloaded at Lerwick in 1949. The Shetland fishermen were paid £3 per cran (about 1,500 fish) and fishing was unlimited for the first two weeks of the season. Fishermen from the mainland of Scotland were restricted in their catches, but received the higher price of 89s. 10d. (almost £4.50) for each cran.

◄ **238**
Cider-making in Gloucestershire. Farmers continued in their old way of life, but the war had brought them greatly increased prosperity.

239
The wife of a farmer in the
Orkneys in 1946.

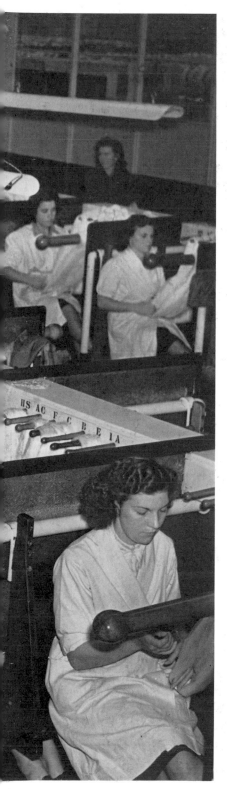

◀ 240
As a result of the war, the textile industry had lost 300,000 workers. In this Doncaster factory in 1948 women were manufacturing rayon from cellulose extracted from cotton waste.

▲ 241
One bright feature of the forties was that unemployment was almost non-existent, but there were the unlucky ones. This Dundee woman worked in a chocolate factory while her husband, unemployed since he had been demobilized two years before, kept house, cooked meals and minded the children. Her wage was £4.10s. a week; his weekly benefit was £1.13s.

242
Londoners going to work by
Underground in one of the
new-style carriages divided
into compartments by glass
partitions and sliding doors,
1947.

▲ **243**
Reconstruction of the blitzed cities proceeded slowly. This bomb fell on a London cinema in 1940 and failed to explode; it was defused and removed in 1949.

▶ **244**
When the bomb was taken away spectators raised 'a ragged but heartfelt cheer', according to the photographer.

▲ 245
Typing class in a Technical College and School of Art. Girls could look forward to a wider variety of jobs than had been available to their mothers.

◄ 246
Nurses, many from West Africa, in 1947.

247
The Women's Press Club,
whose members included
most of Fleet Street's top
women journalists.

▲ **248**
Models from the Gaby
Young Mannequin Agency
hoping to be selected for an
assignment.

▲ **249**
A familiar job with a new
name and a new status – one
of the first Home Helps,
1946.

▲ **250**
Fish and chips for women farm workers on a chilly March day 1948. The van is a converted government ambulance.

▶ **251**
Old crafts survived. In Clerkenwell a spinner and weaver made tassels, loops and fringes for the curtains of Clarence House, the London Home of Princess Elizabeth and the Duke of Edinburgh.

▲ 252
Choosing an umbrella in 1948. This shop survives today.

◀ 253
There were still fifty lamplighters employed in London in 1949. Their work started about three o'clock in the morning during mid-summer. These lamps were in Tower Bridge Road; the bridge can be seen in the background.

▶ **254**
Derby Council at work, 1946.

▼ **255**
The London Stock Exchange, where silk hats were still to be seen.

◄ 256

Friday night in the Stock Exchange. Its floor (18,500 square feet of it) was swept every night and washed every Friday by an army of charwomen.

► 257

By the end of the forties things were looking up. At this canteen in the Isle of Grain refinery, dinners were one shilling and the wall notice stated: 'If you want more potatoes, please ask for them.'

▼ 258

In Petticoat Lane there was no shortage by 1950 of 'Fancy Silk Briefs, only 2s. 6d.'

◀ **259**
From the end of the war
until about 1952–3, Britain's
economy was in a
permanent state of crisis. In
this photograph an
American army sergeant
was buying a newspaper in
Trafalgar Square during the
sterling crisis of 1947. By
1948 Marshall Aid was
pouring into Europe.

▶ **260**
Sir Stafford Cripps
announced the devaluation
of the pound on 19
September 1949. Brokers
had to do their business in
Throgmorton Street,
outside the Stock Exchange,
which was closed for the day.

◄ 261
These miners were congratulating themselves on record production at the end of 1946, but the coal shortage was acute.

▼ 262
By early 1947 the hard winter, the run-down state of the mines and the lack of transport to move the coal, combined to bring Britain to a standstill. Comedians Laurel and Hardy, on a visit in February 1947, found themselves queuing for ration cards — by candlelight.

263
The disastrous winter of 1947 was followed by floods, which in some places cut off the water supply.

▲ **264**
Coal was desperately short
all over Europe. In Dublin
mountains of peat were
stacked in Phoenix Park.

▶ **265**
January 1947 – a German
prisoner-of-war shovelling
snow off a farmhouse roof in
Perthshire.

▲ 266
Housewives queuing for food put on a brave face for the camera. In 1947 every woman in Britain was spending at least one hour of every day waiting in a queue.

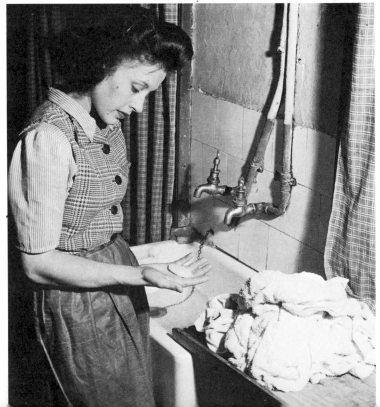

◀ 267
Mothers with young babies received an extra ration of soap for the nappies, but there was not enough.

268
The cold was all the harder
to bear because of the lack
of nourishment, particularly
fats. The 1948 ration was
one ounce of cooking fat
per person per week. This
cupboard, photographed in
1946, was typical of
thousands of British larders.
Even dried eggs had
disappeared from the shops;
the packet in the picture had
been hoarded. At one village
raffle the prize was a solitary
fresh egg.

◀ **269**
At the greengrocer, 1947 –
'No fruit of any kind'.

▼ **270**
Few toys at Selfridges,
Christmas 1946.

▶ 271
The fight for food was hampered by the appalling weather. Farmers ploughed by night to catch up after the long winter.

▼ 272
'Don't ask for bread unless you really want it'.

273
Spring 1947: sowing the
corn by hand on land still too
wet for machinery after the
melting of the snow. Bread
was rationed from 21 July
1946; this had never
happened during the war.

◄ 274
Road verges were ploughed,
sown with barley and
harvested, on the Barnet
By-pass in Middlesex, 1948.

▼ 275
A man 'scything an entry' for
the reaper binder into a field
of wheat — the headland was
too precious to be wasted.

276
This butcher's customers
felt themselves lucky to get
their full meat ration, which
in 1948 was thirteen ounces
per week for the average
man.

▶ 277
A tin of the reviled Snoek, a barracuda-type fish, which in spite of the vigorous promotion by the Government from 1947 to 1948 was too disagreeable for even hungry Britain to swallow.

▼ 278
Housewives queuing for potatoes in the summer of 1947. By 1948 the daily rations were well below wartime level.

◄ 279
Petrol for private use was almost unobtainable from 1947 to 1948, even on the black market. Petrol could easily be tested for the presence of a chemical which could prove whether it was for private use or had been acquired illegally.

▼ 280
A local dance orchestra was transported entirely by bicycle – December 1947.

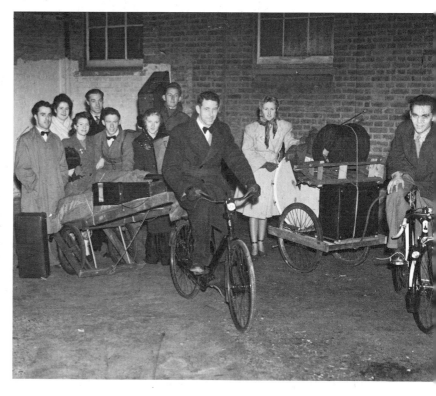

281
Without cars or petrol,
people went on holiday by
train: Waterloo Station in
July 1948.

282
Saleswomen crowding to deal with the rush at the nylon counter in Selfridges, December 1946.

283
In an effort to control the black market 'Spivs and Drones', the Registration for Employment Order came into force in January 1948; street sellers were obliged to 'sign on' at the Labour Exchange.

◀ **284**
A hawker selling nylons illegally, on the pavements in Oxford Street. Look-out men were posted to warn of the arrival of police.

▼ **285**
Sometimes the police got there first.

▲ **286**
Queues became part of the
British way of life, this paper
queue was photographed at
Bala in Wales, 1950.

▶ **287**
In 1949 some goods came
off the ration, but as Sir
Stafford Cripps, then
Chancellor, said: 'Our own
consumption requirements
have to be the last on the list
of priorities.' Rationing did
not disappear finally until
meat came off the ration in
July 1954.

TIME OFF

◀ **288**
 Going for a stroll down a
 London street.

▶ **289**
 Lunch at a Surrey hotel.

▼ **290**
 Ramblers' picnic in
 Savernake Forest.

▼ **291**
Village school children
walking home.

▶ **292**
Whit Monday at the bar of
the Palace Hotel, Southend.

▲ **293**
A Lyons Corner House.

▶ **294**
Locals and visitors at the
Prospect of Whitby in
London's East End.

▲ **295**
Covent Garden workers
were able to enjoy an early
morning pint.

▶ **296**
The Ritz in 1950.

◄ 297
The craze for pin-tables was
denounced by the Press as
being responsible for
juvenile crime.

▼ 298
'Cupid's Secret' – revealed
for one penny in the slot.

▲ **299**
In the north-east, a miners' parade was enjoyed by the whole community.

▶ **300**
Arsenal v. Manchester United, 1946.

◀ **301**
Princess Elizabeth married
the Duke of Edinburgh in
1947; two spectators from
Clapham were determined
to have a good view.

▶ **302**
The Princess was given one
hundred coupons for her
wedding. The silk for the
wedding dress was woven at
Braintree by the Royal
Weavers.

▼ **303**
Another royal occasion: the
Silver Wedding Anniversary
of George VI and Queen
Elizabeth in 1948.

▲ **304**
Etonian and sisters watching
the Fourth of June cricket.

▶ **305**
Speech Day at Harrow.

◄ 306
Debutantes at Queen
Charlotte's Ball, 1952,
dressed in the traditional
white, with the giant
birthday cake.

◄ 307
Buckingham Palace Garden
Party in 1949.

► 308
Off to Ascot, 1948.

▲ **309**
Father minds baby on Brighton beach.

◀ **310**
The original Mrs Mopp, famous as the charwoman in Tommy Handley's *ITMA* radio programme, outside her seaside cafe at Deal.

▲ 311
Bournemouth, 1946.

▶ 312
A thousand holiday makers
could eat simultaneously at
Butlin's Holiday Camp,
Clacton-on-Sea.

◀ **313**
A meet of the Crowhurst Otter Hounds. The Senior Master, on crutches, had held the post for 47 years. His daughter, on the right, was joint master. His wife is seen on his left.

▲ **314**
Farm workers' cinema, 1949.

▼ **315**
The County Library opened once a week at the village shop in Chilham.

▲ 316
Fêtes were sometimes opened by celebrities. This one at Dartford was opened by actress Patricia Dainton; in the queue for her autograph was Miss Margaret Roberts, now Mrs Margaret Thatcher.

◀ 317
The Hokey Cokey at the Nuffield Centre in London.

▲ **318**
Windmill Girls in 1946.

▶ **319**
Cecil Beaton as theatrical designer in 1950.

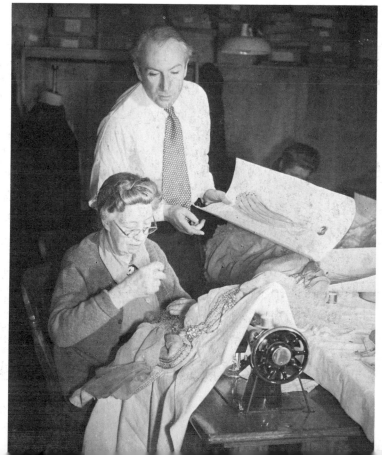

323

The foreign allowance was pathetically meagre, but some people had friends abroad who gave them hospitality. The lucky few could get away for a holiday abroad on the *Queen Elizabeth* or the *Queen Mary*, which still ploughed their stately way across the Atlantic.

324

Dressing for dinner aboard the *Queen Elizabeth*, 1946.

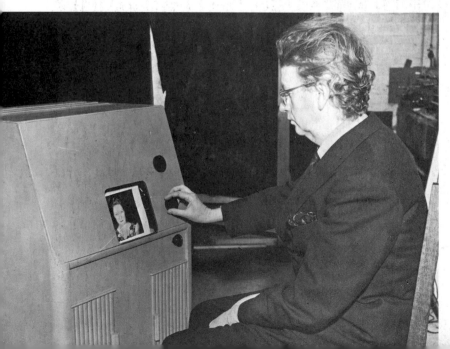

325

John Logie Baird, seen here in the forties, had invented television in the twenties but the war stopped television broadcasting for seven years. The service re-opened on 7 June 1946. London's Victory Parade was televised, Philip Harben demonstrated cookery and Miss Jasmine Bligh came back as an announcer. Most screens were only seven inches wide. In 1947 there were less than 14,000 licence holders; by 1951 there were nearly 800,000.

THE NEW BRITAIN

326
Churchill in 1950. Labour
was exhausted by the
post-war revolution.
Churchill and the Tories lost
in 1950, but came back in the
1951 election.

327
Herbert Morrison and
Clement Attlee at the
Labour Party conference in
1950.

◀ **328**
The Welfare State was the theme of Labour's electoral campaign in that year.

▼ **329**
Rest time at a Woolwich nursery school in 1947.

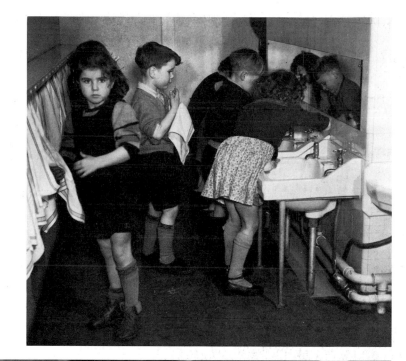

▶ **330**
  The washroom of a primary school in London's Woolwich, 1951, complete with hot and cold running water, soap and towels.

▼ **331**
  School milk and school meals were provided from 1947.

332
Bevan's National Health Scheme was authorized by a bill which became law on 6 November 1946 and came into operation in 1948.

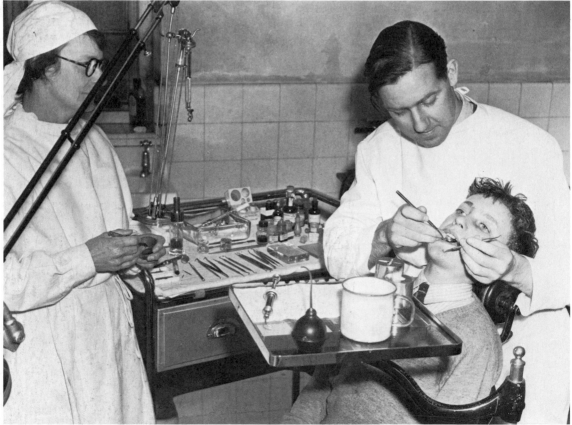

▶ **333**
Fireside and television,
1950.

▶ **334**
'End Your Washday
Drudgery' – one of the first
launderettes.

▶ **335**
This self-service store still
possessed brass scales for
weighing purchases in 1949.

336
Trams finally disappeared
from London on 5 July 1952.
(The last to run was number
1951 on route 40.)

337
The balloon went up at the
Festival of Britain, 1951,
from the River Walk, beside
Powell and Moya's
spectacular Skylon.

338
The Festival in full swing.

◀ **339**
Foundation for the New
Look, 1948. Pads on
shoulders and hips
emphasized a tiny waist.

▶ **340**
Selecting a girl to model
15-denier nylons in 1953.

▶ **341**
A Soho nightclub, The
Pigalle, in 1950.

▲ 342
Women campaigned to share in the growing affluence in 1952.

◀ 343
Teddy boys.

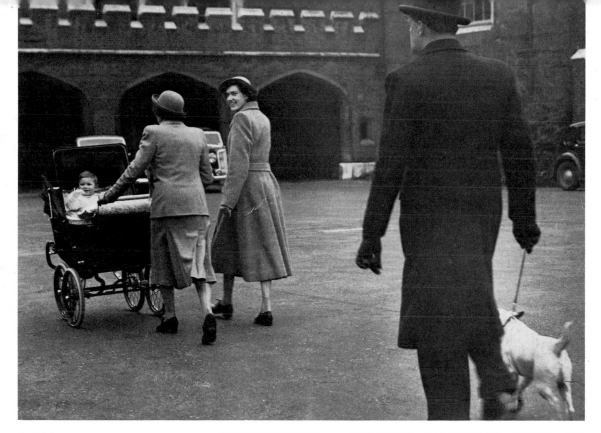

▲ **344**
Prince Charles and his entourage in 1949.

▶ **345**
George VI died in 1952. People all over the country kept a two-minute silence on the day of the funeral.

346
Coronation year, 1953,
started badly with disastrous
floods.

◄ **347**
Cleaning up Lord Nelson
in readiness for the
Coronation celebrations.

▶ **348**
Coronation Day, 2 June 1953.

▶ **349**
The news that Hillary and Tensing had been the first to reach the summit of Mount Everest reached England on Coronation morning.

350
The Queen and Prince Philip
returning from Westminster
Abbey. The heavy rain failed
to dampen the enthusiasm of
New Elizabethans.